Daily Affirmations for Spiritual Empowerment and Growth

Written By
Dr. Robert L. Gaines

LEEDS PUBLISHING HOUSE
CHRISTIAN
WWW.LEEDSBOOKSTORE.COM

ISBN 979-8-89619-363-0
Copyright 2024 © Dr. Robert L. Gaines

This book provides accurate and authoritative information regarding the subject matter covered. This information is given to us to understand that neither the author nor LEEDS PRESS CORP is engaged in rendering legal or professional advice. The opinions expressed by the author are not necessarily those of LEEDS PRESS CORP

Copyright 2024 © Dr. Robert L. Gaines
Cover copyright 2024 © Leeds Press Corp
Cover Design by Leeds Graphics.
Written by Dr. Robert L. Gaines
Edited by Leeds Press Corp, Staff.

Leeds Press Corp encourages the right to free expression and the importance of copyright. The objective of copyright is to encourage authors and artists to produce innovative works that strengthen our society. **Daily Affirmations for Spiritual Empowerment and Growth**...is a LEEDS PRESS CORP publication. The opinions expressed by the author are not necessarily those of LEEDS PRESS CORP. No part of this publication may be reproduced, stored in a retrieval system, or transmitted by any means, electronic, mechanical, photocopy, recording, or otherwise, without the author's prior permission except as provided by USA copyright law. If you would like permission to use material from the book (other than for review purposes), please contact info@leedspress.com.

Leedspublishing.com
Twitter.com/leedspresscorp
Instagram.com/leedspresscorp
Facebook.com/leedspresscorp

LP Books is an imprint of LEEDS PRESS CORP. Name and Logo trademark of LEEDS PRESS CORP. The publisher is not responsible for websites (or their content) that the publisher does not own. LEEDS PRESS SPEAKERS' AGENCY provides a wide range of authors for speaking events.

To find out more; info@leedspress.com or call 323-230-0062 Printed in the United States of America.

Table of Contents

DEDICATION

I would like to dedicate this book to my wife Wanda (My Maria). Thank you for your unwavering love, support and prayers for all these years!

My wonderful sister Mary Jean Johnson who showed me the importance of speaking God's Word and living it out! I'll also like to honor my spiritual family (Greater New Birth Jerusalem Ministries) and friends (We've been there for each other), of impeccable love and character like Christ.

And finally, to my spiritual parents Dr. Robert L. & Anna M. Cook. What a spiritual legacy you laid all for the Father's glory, present with the Lord but never forgotten!

Glory to God!

FOREWORD

Everyone wants to "Have a Great Day". I do not personally know anyone who prefers a bad day. Therefore, this publication is a prayer, a wish, an inspiration, and an encouragement that a great day awaits you. In a time of tensions and divisions in the country and around the world, it is good to know that we can turn to this masterfully crafted book of inspiration by Dr. Robert Gaines. This publication reminds me of Apostle Paul's writing, in 3 John 1:2 "Beloved, I wish above all things that thou mayest prosper and be in health, even as thy soul prospereth."

"Have a Great Day Today" can be spoken over other people's lives as a prayer, including our loved ones and one's own personal life on a daily basis as well. The power of the spoken words cannot be over emphasized for, "Death and life are in the power of the tongue" according to Proverbs 18:21.

"Have A Great Day Today" is a positive way to verbally pronounce a blessing on a person, a spouse, a child, or a friend.

Bishop George O. Adebanjo, Th.D.
Founder, The Living Word International Church, Nashville, Tn.
Author

PART I

Embracing Divine Strength

"Have a Great Day Today! Remember, the divine strength of God is within you. This strength empowers you to achieve what only God can manifest through your actions. Stand bold in service to the Greater One inside you. Resist the temptation to conform to worldly ways. Remember, the biggest hurdles you face are those you set for yourself. Keep your focus strong and move forward with determination."

Trust in Jesus Christ's Boundless Capability

"Have a Great Day Today! Whatever your worries or challenges, believe in the words of Ephesians 3:20 – Jesus Christ can do immeasurably more than we ask or imagine. Trust in His boundless capability to guide and aid you."

Proclaiming God's Favor

"Have a Great Day Today! Join me in declaring, 'God is working for my benefit. His favor surrounds me!' as stated in Romans 8:28. Affirm this truth to feel the shift in your spirit."

The Presence of the Holy Spirit

"Have a Great Day Today! Be aware that the Holy Spirit, who resurrected Jesus, is also within us. This presence guides us beyond mere sensory satisfaction – what we see, hear, touch, taste, and smell. Keep your focus, knowing He is with you. Let the joy of the Lord Jesus, the love of God, and the fellowship of the Holy Spirit (2 Corinthians 13:14) be with you."

Guidance Through Challenges

"Have a Great Day Today! If you feel like you're in turmoil, it's time to retrace your steps. Consult the ultimate guide – the Bible – to correct your path and continue with divine guidance."

The Power of Faith Over Emotions

"Have a Great Day Today! Remember, faith transcends emotions and propels us forward, even in the thickest battles. It connects us to God's eternal promises (Hebrews 12:2). Our spoken words reflect our deepest beliefs. Speak strength, not weakness; success, not failure, as E.W. Kenyon suggests."

Renewing Mind and Spirit

"Have a Great Day Today! Let's cleanse our hearts and minds from doubts, fears, and disbelief in God's extraordinary power. Align our thoughts with the truth of His Word (Romans 12:2), allowing for a transformation of mind and spirit."

Recognizing the Power of Words

"Have a Great Day Today! Beware of the deception that our words are powerless. Jesus taught that His words are life-giving and spiritually potent (John 6:63). May God grant you unique advantages and opportunities. Remember, actions speak louder than words, and our thoughts, words, and meditations greatly matter (Proverbs 23:7, James 3:2-18). Stay firmly focused on your path."

Transformation Through Jesus

"Have a Great Day Today! The journey is not about self-improvement but entrusting our transformation to Jesus. Shift your focus from self to God's transformative power. The Holy Spirit enlivens what Jesus achieved for us (John 16:13-15). By embracing truth, your mind becomes purified (1 Peter 1:22). Guard your heart, for it is precious."

Embracing Victory in the Lord

"Have a Great Day Today! Remember, no plan or wisdom can prevail against the Lord. Victory lies with Him (Proverbs 21:30-31). Live fully now; don't wait for 'someday.' Pray, prepare, plan, and pursue. Take your dreams beyond just thoughts – Hart Ramsey's words remind us not to carry our dreams to the grave."

PART II

Praising to Find Peace

"Have a Great Day Today! Redirect your focus from worries to worship. Praise the Lord until He becomes your sole focus. Remember, God's promises are unchangeable as declared in Psalm 119:89. Commit to speaking righteousness, as in Psalm 17:3. Just as God blessed Abraham, He blesses you. Speak positivity for transformation!"

Wishing Prosperity and Health

"Have a Great Day Today! My prayer for you is prosperity and good health, mirroring the wellness of your soul, as hoped for in 3 John 2. Embrace and receive this blessing!"

Faith as a Catalyst for Success

"Have a Great Day Today! Let faith elevate you beyond past failures, leading you to a life filled with success and prosperity."

Rising Through Confession

"Have a Great Day Today! Realize that we won't exceed our own confessions. Seek a 'secret place' for deep spiritual connection and intimacy with God. This is where you activate your spiritual essence over the physical."

Giving Voice to God's Promises

"Have a Great Day Today! Speak God's promises aloud; this action prompts angelic beings to align with His will (Hebrews 1:14, Psalm 103:20). Your faithful declarations activate divine plans."

Embracing Righteousness in Christ

"Have a Great Day Today! With Christ in your life, your spirit has received eternal life and righteousness, as stated in Romans 8:10. You bear God's righteousness within."

Faith Unhindered by Doubt

"Have a Great Day Today! Avoid letting doubt, rooted in worldly views, undermine your faith. Stay steadfast in your beliefs and maintain a strong focus on God's Word."

Pursuing Your Divine Purpose

"Have a Great Day Today! Dismiss doubts and never compromise on your God-given purpose. Your dreams are valuable; persist in your faith and fight for them."

Overcoming Setbacks

"Have a Great Day Today! Don't let minor setbacks deter you. Recognize the greatness within you and keep moving forward."

Embracing the Word for Overcoming Adversity

"Have a Great Day Today! Regularly engaging with the Word of God shapes your thoughts, equipping you to triumph over challenges. Remember, correct knowledge empowers you to be victorious (Romans 8:37)."

Choosing God Fully

"Have a Great Day Today! Realize that limiting God to parts of your life hinders His full blessings. Embrace Him completely for a fulfilling and enriched life journey. Live fully in His way, for it is the superior path."

PART III

Experiencing Life in Christ

"Have a Great Day Today! Consider how you are when influenced by substances like alcohol or drugs. Now, imagine being 'intoxicated' with the spirit of Jesus. Embrace this spiritual high and let others see the joy and fulfillment it brings, as Tom Loud suggests."

Recognizing God's Sufficiency

"Have a Great Day Today! Realize that having God means you have everything. Affirm with confidence, 'God is my more than enough!' as stated in Philippians 4:19."

The Power of Speaking God's Word

"Let the spoken Word impact the atmosphere, silencing any negativity or criticism. Remember, God's provision is abundant; He cared for millions in the wilderness, and He will care for you too."

Living in Victory Through Jesus

"Have a Great Day Today! Just as Jesus overcame the world (John 16:33), so have you. Prioritize seeking God's kingdom and righteousness (Matthew 6:33), embrace the spirit of adoption (Romans 8:15), and act on God's instructions to grow in confidence (James 1:22). Remember, God is committed to completing His good work in you."

Living Set Apart for God

"Have a Great Day Today! The Spirit of God calls us to a life dedicated to Him, distinct from sin. As in Acts 20:32, commit to a life filled with God's power and anointing."

Trusting in the Power of God's Word

"Have a Great Day Today! Strengthen your confidence in God's Word, understanding that no word from Him is powerless. He is faithful to fulfill His promises."

Understanding Faith as a Substance

"Have a Great Day Today! Recognize faith as a tangible substance within you (Hebrews 11:1). It acts as evidence of unseen hopes, drawing these aspirations closer to reality."

Declaring to Receive God's Provision

"Have a Great Day Today! Acknowledge that God has already provided for your needs. Declare your faith openly, allowing God to manifest these provisions. Your life aligns with your dominant thoughts, so focus on God's promises and truths."

Living for Christ

"Have a Great Day Today! In response to Jesus' sacrifice (2 Corinthians 5:21), commit to living your life for Him. Stay focused on this purpose."

Acting from Inner Conviction

"Have a Great Day Today! Reflect on how your thoughts and actions demonstrate your identity and purpose. God wants us to live proactively, from our inner convictions, rather than being swayed by external circumstances."

PART IV

Embracing the Power of Positive Confession

"Have a Great Day Today! Remember, biblical confession is about affirming God's Word, bearing witness to its truths and declarations. Engage in this practice to align yourself with the promises and teachings of Scripture."

Guiding Your Thoughts Toward Positivity

"Have a Great Day Today! Your life follows your most dominant thoughts. Regularly reflect on your thinking patterns. Focusing on God's Word (Proverbs 23:7a) will lead to positive transformations."

Understanding Faith as a Tangible Force

"Have a Great Day Today! Faith, a 'substance' of hope (Hebrews 11:1), is a dynamic force within you. Utilize it as evidence of unseen aspirations, drawing them closer to your reality."

Living Authentically from Within

"Have a Great Day Today! Your thoughts and actions reveal your true self. God encourages living from the inside out, acting on your beliefs rather than reacting to external pressures. Embrace your uniqueness, as Hart Ramsey advises – originality is always more valued than imitation."

Staying Committed to God's Path

"Have a Great Day Today! Saying 'yes' to God means unwavering commitment, even when things don't go as expected. Don't revert to old ways; stay on the path God has set for you."

Acknowledging God as Your Sufficiency

"Have a Great Day Today! If you have God, you have everything. Declare, 'God is my more than enough!' (Philippians 4:19). Don't let others' limitations hinder your dreams. Align with God's Word and watch your life flourish."

Finding Goodness in Difficulty

"Have a Great Day Today! In tough times, affirm, 'God is good, and He does good' (Psalm 119:68). Trust that good will emerge. Don't be deterred by others' opinions when you choose your path."

Cultivating Positivity

"Have a Great Day Today! Strive to remain positive in all circumstances. God promises to work for our good in all situations (Romans 8:28). Keep this focus."

Shaping Your Destiny Through Thoughts and Actions

"Have a Great Day Today! Monitor your thoughts, for they become words, and choose your words carefully as they lead to actions. Your actions form habits, which develop your character and ultimately shape your destiny."

Holding Fast to Your Faith

"Have a Great Day Today! As instructed in Hebrews 4:14, steadfastly hold onto your confession of faith. Constantly affirm the revelations God has provided to you."

Navigating Life's Challenges with Faith

"Have a Great Day Today! Be prepared for life's trials, including major changes and unanswered prayers, as Rick Warren suggests. These are tests of faith and resilience."

Embracing the Transformation Through Faith

"Have a Great Day Today! Engage in the divine exchange: your sins for Christ's righteousness. Seek a church that preaches God's Word and go with expectation. Remember, the Bible emphasizes a relationship with a living, loving God. You are as close to God as you choose to be (Psalm 145:18). Stay devoted and expectant."

Unifying Belief and Speech

"Have a Great Day Today! Your belief system should align with your speech (Romans 10:8-10). Let your words reflect your faith and convictions."

PART V

Aligning Beliefs and Speech

"Have a Great Day Today! Your beliefs and words are intertwined (Romans 10:8-10). Speak in harmony with your faith, affirming your convictions with the power of your words."

Self-Reflection for Personal Growth

"Have a Great Day Today! Consider if your current circumstances are a reflection of your own attitudes and actions. Self-awareness can be a key to unlocking personal growth."

The Essence of Confession

"Have a Great Day Today! Confession in the spiritual context means echoing God's words and promises from the Bible. It's an act of agreement with His divine truths."

Defining Success in God's Kingdom

"Have a Great Day Today! Success in God's eyes isn't about earthly gains but faithfulness and obedience (Matthew 25:23). Measure your success by your devotion and commitment."

Exercising Patience and Forgiveness

"Have a Great Day Today! Let patience anchor you, not your circumstances. Treat others with kindness, regardless of how they treat you. Pray through your pain, forgive, and live your life fully - as Hart Ramsey advises."

Stepping into God's Plan with Faith

"Have a Great Day Today! The challenges you face cannot derail God's plan for you. Venture into the unknown with faith, knowing that God's plans involve your active participation (Isaiah 46:10-11)."

Embracing God's Language of Possibility

"Have a Great Day Today! Erase 'I can't' from your vocabulary. Align your speech with God's word, focusing on eternal truths over fleeting worldly desires (1 John 2:17)."

The Joy of the Holy Spirit

"Have a Great Day Today! The Holy Spirit within us is a promise of our eternal inheritance (Ephesians 1:13-14). Find happiness in your relationship with God, as it is a choice that only you can make (Psalm 37:4)."

The Power of Words and Faith

"Have a Great Day Today! Be mindful of your speech as it can set off unintended consequences (James 3:5-6). Strengthen your faith through daily meditation on God's Word (Joshua 1:8) for success in life."

Living According to God's Standard

"Have a Great Day Today! Make a firm decision to live by God's Word. Remember, every experience has a purpose, and God works through our struggles (Romans 16:20). Trust in His plan, even in darkness."

Declaring Blessings and Peace

"Have a Great Day Today! I declare in Jesus' Name, may the Lord bless and keep you, shine upon you, favor you, and grant you peace."

Activating Divine Favor

"Have a Great Day Today! Divine favor is God's goodness towards you. Activate this favor by obedience to God's Word (Jeremiah 29:11). With God's favor, nothing is impossible."

Gaining Divine Wisdom and Insight

"Have a Great Day Today! Beyond skills and knowledge, seek the heart and mind of God (Dr. Bill Winston). With His wisdom, utilize your abilities to fulfill your divine calling."

Overcoming Life's Challenges with Faith

"Have a Great Day Today! Like a sheep bitten by a snake, remember that the venom of life's challenges can't overcome the power of the Lamb's blood. Stay strong in faith, unaffected by life's bites."

PART VI

Valuing Scripture for Guidance

"Have a Great Day Today! Acknowledge the profound inspiration of Scripture, essential for teaching, correcting, and training in righteousness (2 Timothy 3:16). Let it guide your path."

Elevating Experience to Align with God's Word

"Have a Great Day Today! If your experiences don't match God's promises, keep faith in His Word. Seek to raise your experiences to the level of His Word, maintaining focus and trust."

Shaping Identity Through Thoughts and Surroundings

"Have a Great Day Today! Remember, the things you think about and surround yourself with mold your identity. Don't let others define you; stay true to your own self."

Unlocking Success with Faith

"Have a Great Day Today! Utilize the key to your success within you (Joshua 1:8). Believe and speak in faith. Release unforgiveness to protect your character and sanity, as advised by Hart Ramsey."

Developing Godly Character

"Have a Great Day Today! Practice righteousness daily, regardless of your feelings. This is how God's character is cultivated within you."

Agreeing with God's Word for True Walk

"Have a Great Day Today! Walk with God by aligning your words and actions with His Word. Aim to do things that inspire others to become better, not just to impress them."

Standing Firm in Faith Against Impossibilities

"Have a Great Day Today! In the face of challenges, hold steadfastly to your faith. Remember, faith often demands the seemingly impossible."

Embracing Growth and Victory in Trials

"Have a Great Day Today! God always has more for us. He promises victory amidst life's trials (John 16:33) and offers grace even in the presence of sin."

Honoring God with Our Bodies and Minds

"Have a Great Day Today! Honor God with your body, the temple of the Holy Spirit (1 Corinthians 6:19). Believe in His mighty power for believers (Ephesians 1:19) and live in a way that reflects His love and grace."

Reaffirming Faith Amidst Challenges

"Have a Great Day Today! Stand firm in your faith, even when facing impossibilities. Faith is about believing in and demanding the miraculous."

Internalizing and Living Jesus' Teachings

"Have a Great Day Today! Embrace Jesus' teachings, letting them deeply influence your heart and mind, so that you live them out each day."

Loving Jesus in All Seasons

"Have a Great Day Today! Love Jesus even when things don't go as expected (Matthew 11:6). Beware of distractions that can harm more than destruction, as Hart Ramsey cautions."

Declaring God's Justice and Completion

"Have a Great Day Today! Declare with conviction: The Lord, as my Avenger, will right every wrong and complete what He started in my life (Psalm 112:6). Trust in His righteous and everlasting remembrance."

PART VII

The Power of Asking and Receiving

"Have a Great Day Today! Remember the promise of Matthew 7:8 – everyone who asks receives, and those who seek find. Prepare for the day of Christ's judgment (2 Corinthians 5:10) and rejoice in being Saved With Amazing Grace (SWAG). Don't be deceived like the devil, trust in God's plan for true happiness and peace. Even in your mistakes, know that God is there to uplift you, as Hart Ramsey reminds."

Believing Shapes Reality

"Have a Great Day Today! Your beliefs shape your reality (Matthew 9:29). Hold onto your faith and expect positive outcomes."

Following the Spirit's Guidance

"Have a Great Day Today! While we may not always understand the Anointing, staying sensitive to the Holy Spirit and immersing in God's Word will guide us to the right conclusions."

Speaking Faith into Existence

"Have a Great Day Today! Thinking and speaking in faith can transform defeat into victory. God responds to our confession of His Word – without it, there is no divine action."

Embracing Change for Growth

"Have a Great Day Today! Don't be bound by tradition; be open to the 'new things' God is doing. Growth requires change and often happens outside of comfort zones. Be brave and step out in faith for growth and change."

Living the Truth of God's Word

"Have a Great Day Today! God's Word is the ultimate truth (John 17:17). Living by this truth daily brings blessings, while negative speech can hinder them. Remember, Jesus overcame all obstacles so you could live in victory."

Walking in Light and Liberty

"Have a Great Day Today! God has already dealt with the devil; it's our turn to live in the light and freedom of His Word. Success is not material wealth but fulfilling your divine purpose."

Transforming Thinking for Destiny

"Have a Great Day Today! Your thoughts can lead to success or failure. Realign your mind with God's perspective and refuse to let past experiences limit your belief in your destiny."

The Importance of Confessing the Word

"Have a Great Day Today! It's not just prayer, but the confession of the Word's truth that brings change. Declare your ability to do what God says you can and affirm your identity as defined by His Word."

Exercising Authority Over Challenges

"Have a Great Day Today! Exercise your authority over life's battles daily, as advised by Apostle Paul (2 Corinthians 10:3-5). Don't allow fear or doubt to dominate; instead, take control and assert your dominion."

PART VIII

Embracing Transformation Through God's Word

"Have a Great Day Today! Reach your divine destiny by letting God's Word transform your thoughts, emotions, decisions, actions, habits, and ultimately, your character."

Living with Spirit-led Attitude

"Have a Great Day Today! Live from within, not labeling life's events as 'good' or 'bad.' Trust in the Holy Spirit to guide you through life's challenges, confident that He will create paths in seemingly impossible situations (Romans 8:28)."

Reframing Thoughts for Destiny

"Have a Great Day Today! Your mindset can lead to success or failure. Shift your thoughts to align with God's vision and don't let past experiences hinder your belief in your destiny."

Realizing the Kingdom Within

"Have a Great Day Today! Recognize that the Kingdom of God resides within you (Luke 17:21). This inner divine presence guides and shapes your life."

Understanding the Purpose of Prayer

"Have a Great Day Today! Prayer is a pathway to knowing God more deeply. Remember, God's actions in your life align with His benevolent will. Impact lives by simply knowing Jesus and loving others, as Hart Ramsey advises."

Embracing Divine Favor

"Have a Great Day Today! Follow Daniel's example, understanding that God's favor can elevate you to places beyond your reach alone. Daily affirm and expect God's favor, envisioning it as a protective shield around you (Daniel 1:9 AMP)."

Trusting God's Plan Despite Uncertainty

"Have a Great Day Today! God's plans for a prosperous future (Jeremiah 29:11-14) may defy logic, but trust in His divine wisdom. Move past the pains and disappointments of yesterday."

Declaring Your Identity in Christ

"Have a Great Day Today! Affirm your identity as more than a victor and an overcomer, a child of God, an heir alongside Christ. Embrace the strength in Philippians 4:13, declaring your ability to do all through Christ."

Countering Satan's Attacks with God's Goodness

"Have a Great Day Today! When Satan tries to cast doubt on God's goodness, silence him with the truth of Psalm 100:5. Remember, you're built without a 'quit switch' – God chose you as a winner."

Overcoming Doubts with Faith in God's Word

"Have a Great Day Today! Base your faith not on feelings but on the unerring Word of God. Reject any thoughts that contradict His Word, recognizing them as falsehoods from the enemy. Equip yourself with knowledge of Satan's character to overcome his deceptions."

PART VIIII

Speaking to Your Challenges

"Have a Great Day Today! Your voice has power over your challenges (Mark 11:23). Be cautious with whom you share your heart, especially with those who have shown disregard for its care."

Finding Life Within

"Have a Great Day Today! Your true essence lies within (Colossians 1:27). Circumstances do not define you. Trust in God's unbreakable promise (Hebrews 6:18) and focus on the life Christ has ignited in you."

Embracing God's Thinking for Success

"Have a Great Day Today! Align your mindset with God's (Philippians 4:8). The success you achieve correlates with the degree to which you accept His way of thinking."

Holding Firm in Faith

"Have a Great Day Today! The Father will manifest as you confess Him to be. If prayers seem unanswered or deliverance delayed, remain steadfast in your confession of faith (Luke 1:37).

Reinforce positive self-talk with God's Word, as Hart Ramsey suggests."

Understanding Kingdom Principles

"Have a Great Day Today! The Kingdom of God operates beyond limitations, a realm of self-sufficiency and abundance (Hebrews 11:6). Faith is the key to experiencing this boundless domain."

Trusting in God's Foreknowledge

"Have a Great Day Today! God is aware of your needs even before you voice them (Matthew 6:8). Trust in His omniscience and care for you."

Confronting Rather Than Denying

"Have a Great Day Today! Avoid denial; it's detrimental. Acknowledge, repent, and forgive to heal emotionally and spiritually. Be mindful of cultural influences that obscure God, seeking Him earnestly (1 Peter 2:24, Philippians 4:6-9)."

The Power of Appropriate Words

"Have a Great Day Today! Words spoken aptly are invaluable (Proverbs 25:11). Let the Holy Spirit guide your speech for a maximized life (Proverbs 13:2,3)."

Decision-Making Aligned with God's Word

"Have a Great Day Today! Base your decisions on God's Word, keeping Him at the forefront (Matthew 6:33). Remember, nothing happens by chance; align your choices with divine guidance."

Responding with Faith Over Time

"Have a Great Day Today! Understand that delays in God's plan are not denials. Choose faith and perseverance over complaint, trusting you're on the right path with God, regardless of timing."

A Prayer for Spiritual Insight

"Have a Great Day Today! I pray for you to be indued with the Spirit of Wisdom and Revelation. May you fully realize what God has accomplished in Christ, your identity in Him, and the riches at your disposal (Ephesians 1:16-23)."

PART X

64

Believing in God's Unseen Favor

"Have a Great Day Today! Trust in God's favor even when it's not visible in the natural world. Our faith allows us to believe and expect His favor, unseen but ever-present (Psalm 5:12)."

The Importance of Daily Prayer

"Have a Great Day Today! Remember to pray, for God graciously granted us another day. Acknowledge His continuous blessings with gratitude and communication."

Focusing on the Future

"Have a Great Day Today! Let go of the past and direct your attention forward. You can't alter what's happened, but you can shape what's to come."

Testing Moral Strength

"Have a Great Day Today! Your moral resolve is truly tested in the face of temptation. Stay steadfast and strong in your values and beliefs."

Finding Happiness in God's Plan

"Have a Great Day Today! The more you align with God's plan, the greater your happiness and peace will be. Trust in His guidance for your life."

Encouraging Yourself in God's Goodness

"Have a Great Day Today! Bolster your confidence by reflecting on God's deeds and kindness (Exodus 34:6). Use His past faithfulness as a source of encouragement."

Overcoming Disappointments

"Have a Great Day Today! View disappointments not as setbacks, but as opportunities for growth and resilience (Jeremiah 17:7). Confidence in Christ, not in self, is key to overcoming life's challenges."

Declaring Blessings on Home and Work

"Have a Great Day Today! Speak blessings over your home and workplace. Embrace opportunities for spiritual growth and recommit to serving God."

Discerning Spiritual Deceptions

"Have a Great Day Today! Be vigilant against justifying wrong actions with misleading spiritual logic. Recognize and understand the enemy's tactics."

Handling Mistakes with Forgiveness

"Have a Great Day Today! When you falter, quickly confess, seek God's forgiveness, and then forgive yourself (2 Chronicles 7:14, 1 John 1:9). Stay focused on growth and redemption."

Embracing Our Role in God's Plan

"Have a Great Day Today! Acknowledge that Christianity involves trusting that God knows and provides for our needs (Matthew 6:8,32). As His chosen, bring His Kingdom to earth through your words and actions. Your faith declarations have the power to manifest reality."

PART IX

Speaking Words of Grace

"Have a Great Day Today! Let your words be a source of grace to others and to yourself. Speak what God says about every aspect of your life to reinforce positive truths."

Protecting Your Joy

"Have a Great Day Today! Safeguard your joy from being stolen by the devil (Proverbs 17:22, Nehemiah 8:10). Remember, the joy of the Lord is your strength, and joyful confession can lead to restoration and abundance (Jeremiah 33:11, Proverbs 6:30-31)."

Being Continually Filled with God's Spirit

"Have a Great Day Today! Seek to be continually filled with God's Spirit to fulfill His will in your life. A single word from God can bring clarity and direction to your confusion."

Speaking Faith Boldly

"Have a Great Day Today! Declare your faith with confidence. Focus on your expectations and let go of your troubled past. Embrace this new season with positivity."

Confession as a Spiritual Law

"Have a Great Day Today! Christianity is often called 'the great confession.' Believe and speak your faith before possession (Romans 10:9-10). Your words have the power to shape your reality."

The Power of Right Confession

"Have a Great Day Today! Your words can either imprison or liberate you (Proverbs 6:2). Speak positively to build strength and freedom in your life."

Trusting in God's Provision

"Have a Great Day Today! Believe that God knows your needs and has already made provision for them (Matthew 6:8,32). Trust in His omniscience and benevolence."

Staying in God's Peace

"Have a Great Day Today! No matter the circumstances, remember God is in control. Maintain peace, knowing His presence is constant in your life."

Declaring God's Plan and Prosperity

"Have a Great Day Today! Proclaim that God has a plan for your day. Expect prosperity and supernatural peace. Remember, Jesus brings life to every situation, even his own funeral!"

Embracing God's Eternal Promises

"Have a Great Day Today! Trust in the eternal nature of God's promises (Psalm 119:89). Focus on these promises, not your problems."

The Power of Confession

"Have a Great Day Today! Boldly confess God's Word to take possession of His promises (Isaiah 55:11). Align your speech with His truth to see His power at work in your life."

Trusting God's Plan in Uncertainty

"Have a Great Day Today! Everything happens for a reason. Trust that God is working all things for good (Romans 8:28, Isaiah 40:8). Ask God for unexpected favor and rejoice in His grace."

Peace in God's Sovereignty

"Have a Great Day Today! Find peace in the knowledge that God's responses to our prayers are part of His perfect control. Live authentically in every aspect of your life."

Taking Action in Faith

"Have a Great Day Today! Faith demands action for results. Act on God's Word confidently, knowing it will never fail."

Being an Instrument of Hope

"Have a Great Day Today! Be a beacon of hope and encouragement. Extend God's love to someone in need and be a bridge to their salvation."

Prayer with Thanksgiving

"Have a Great Day Today! Pray with thanksgiving, acknowledging that what you have asked for is already done (Philippians 4:6,7). Gratitude is a key component of faith."

PART XII

Embracing Forgiveness and Letting Go

"Have a Great Day Today! Choose to forgive, regardless of whether an apology has been offered. Remember, you have the power to let go and rise above bitterness."

Sustaining on God's Word

"Have a Great Day Today! Live not just by physical sustenance but by every word of God (Luke 4:4). Let His teachings guide and focus your life."

Reflecting God's Image

"Have a Great Day Today! Remember, you're made in God's image. Reflect His character in your words and actions. Beware of bitterness; it's a choice, often fueled by unforgiveness."

Praying with Thanksgiving

"Have a Great Day Today! Pray with thanksgiving, believing that your requests are already fulfilled (Philippians 4:6,7). Gratitude amplifies the power of prayer."

Celebrating Life's Simple Pleasures

"Have a Great Day Today! Appreciate the ultimate sacrifice of Jesus Christ. Start and end your day in prayer, and be thankful for life's simple joys. May those who doubted you witness your celebration and honor."

Building a Foundation for Success

"Have a Great Day Today! Success requires a solid foundation of knowledge, understanding, and wisdom (Proverbs 2:11-12, 16:22, 14:35). These are the cornerstones for enduring achievements and happiness."

Developing in God's Love

"Have a Great Day Today! Grow in God's love, letting it influence your thoughts, speech, and actions. Share your faith actively to understand the goodness in Christ (Philemon 1:6). Seek peace and prosperity through God (Job 22:21). Remember, Christ is within you."

Trusting God's Constant Presence

"Have a Great Day Today! In all situations, know that God is in control. Maintain peace, assured of His unending presence with you."

Making Positive Confessions

"Have a Great Day Today! Your words can transform your life. Speak positively and faithfully, as this shapes your reality. Avoid negative or neutral confessions; it's the positive, clear-cut declarations that lead to victories."

Speaking Life Through Words

"Have a Great Day Today! Your words have the power to reach places where other resources can't. Speak God's Word in every situation. Remember, God always provides solutions to the challenges He allows in your life."

Embracing God's Unfailing Love

"Have a Great Day Today! Recognize the value God places on you, demonstrated through Christ's sacrifice. Trust in His unwavering love to meet all your needs today."

PART XIII

Embracing Forgiveness and God's Value for Us

"Have a Great Day Today! Forgive freely and remember your immense value to God, as shown through Christ's sacrifice. Reflect His teachings in your life (John 14:24, Psalm 116:1)."

Trusting in God's Salvation and Strength

"Have a Great Day Today! Affirm your trust in God, your unwavering source of strength and salvation (Isaiah 12:2)."

Overcoming Adversity with God's Favor

"Have a Great Day Today! Know that God's favor is with you, even in adversity (Psalm 41:11). Use His strength to overcome past disappointments and embrace new opportunities."

Knowing and Receiving God's Word

"Have a Great Day Today! Be aware of what God's Word says about your circumstances. When you align your actions with His teachings, God will act in your favor."

Sensitivity to God's Anointing

"Have a Great Day Today! Seek a deeper connection with God to understand His anointing. Ask Him to remove any distractions and dedicate yourself to serving Him."

Discovering God's Plans Through Prayer

"Have a Great Day Today! Dedicate time to prayer to uncover God's plans. Trust that He will guide your steps when you seek His will."

Speaking God's Word in Faith

"Have a Great Day Today! Fill your heart with God's Word so that your faith, not your feelings, will guide your life. Prayer is about speaking His Word and listening for His guidance."

Choosing God Over Feelings

"Have a Great Day Today! Prioritize God's Word over your feelings. Stay committed to His teachings to navigate life faithfully."

Guarding Our Words

"Have a Great Day Today! Be mindful of your speech (Psalm 141:3 AMP). Speak in alignment with God's favor and avoid negative confessions."

Reliance on God in All Situations

"Have a Great Day Today! Remember, through faith in God, you can endure anything. Rely on Him for strength in every circumstance."

Ruling with God's Authority

"Have a Great Day Today! Believe in your authority as a ruler in God's kingdom. Speak with conviction to release His power in your life - as Pastor Bill Winston teaches."

Rejoicing in God's Goodness

"Have a Great Day Today! Reflect on God's blessings (Psalm 107:15). Avoid jealousy and celebrate God's work in others' lives - as Hart Ramsey advises."

Trusting God's Purpose

"Have a Great Day Today! Trust that everything works together for your good if you love God (Romans 8:28). Praise, seek, worship, trust, and thank God in every moment."

Confessing God's Favor

"Have a Great Day Today! Confess God's favor in your life (Romans 8:28). Share your struggles with Him, not for judgment, but for enlightenment and empowerment."

Prioritizing God's Word and Obedience

"Have a Great Day Today! Live by God's spiritual laws, seeking Him first (Matthew 6:33). Let your faith in Him guide your understanding and guard your heart as you await His promises (Philippians 3:10)."

The Power of Prayer

"Have a Great Day Today! Recognize the immense power of prayer. Don't wait for problems to seek God. Constantly remind Him of His promises."

Feeding Faith Over Fear

"Have a Great Day Today! Overcome distractions and failure by feeding your faith, not your fears. Be uplifted and reassured by God's Word."

Defining Yourself by God's Word

"Have a Great Day Today! Remember, you are not defined by feelings, fears, or failures. Let God's Word be your ultimate reality and definition."

PART XIV

Declaring Victory Through God's Word

"Have a Great Day Today! Rise above your circumstances by finding and declaring God's promises of victory. Remember, finding God brings life and favor (Proverbs 8:35-36). Let go of hurts and focus on God's healing Word."

Creating Tomorrow with Today's Words

"Have a Great Day Today! Your words today shape your world tomorrow. Choose them carefully to cultivate a blessed and fulfilling life."

Responding with Faith to Life's Situations

"Have a Great Day Today! Your spirit responds to your confession of faith. Remember, faith is born in the spirit, not in reasoning. Let your confession reflect your faith in God."

Speaking to Obstacles with Authority

"Have a Great Day Today! Believe in the power of your words as well as God's. Speak to your challenges with faith and authority, as Jesus taught us (Mark 11:23)."

Trusting Despite Doubts

"Have a Great Day Today! When doubts arise, affirm your belief in God. Trust in Him even when understanding is elusive."

Encouraging Others in Faith

"Have a Great Day Today! Be an encourager, infusing courage into others' hearts. Encourage them to embrace godliness and reject despair (Hebrews 10:25)."

Declaring Your Identity in Christ

"Have a Great Day Today! Proclaim your identity in God's love: beloved, empowered, and guided by Christ. Face challenges with the strength He provides (2 Timothy 1:7)."

Guarding Your Speech for God's Favor

"Have a Great Day Today! Mind your words and speak in alignment with God's favor (Psalm 141:3 AMP). Your speech can attract God's blessings in your life."

Enduring Through Faith in God

"Have a Great Day Today! Endure any situation with reliance on God. With faith in Him, you can overcome anything."

Speaking as a Son of God

"Have a Great Day Today! Speak with the authority of a child of God. When you decree, Heaven and earth respond to your words."

Appreciating Life's Blessings

"Have a Great Day Today! Find joy in life's small blessings. Recognize the abundance you already have."

Seeking Divine Guidance in Decision Making

"Have a Great Day Today! Make decisions guided by God's Word (Matthew 6:33). Remember, divine guidance leads to lasting success and fulfillment."

Embracing Prayer as a Powerful Tool

"Have a Great Day Today! Acknowledge prayer as your most powerful resource. Connect with God regularly, not just in times of trouble."

Feeding Faith Over Fear

"Have a Great Day Today! Starve your fears and nourish your faith. Rise above distractions and failure by focusing on God's promises."

Defining Yourself by God's Word

"Have a Great Day Today! Identify yourself through God's Word, not by your emotions or circumstances. You are defined by His truth and love."

Committing to God's Word for Abundant Life

"Have a Great Day Today! Commit wholeheartedly to obeying God's Word. This commitment opens the door to an abundant life filled with His blessings."

Living as a Testament to God's Love

"Have a Great Day Today! Live in a way that brings others to God. Rest in His promises, knowing He is a covenant-keeping God."

Choosing Your Focus Wisely

"Have a Great Day Today! Focus on God's kingdom first (Matthew 6:33). Surround yourself with relationships that fuel this focus for long-term success."

Speaking Blessings and Overcoming Obstacles

"Have a Great Day Today! Declare blessings over your life. Believe in the miracle-working power of God's Word to overcome every challenge you face."

Participating Actively in God's Plan

"Have a Great Day Today! Engage actively in God's plan. Use your faith and words to unlock His extraordinary works in your life."

Overcoming Challenges with a Renewed Mind

"Have a Great Day Today! Transform challenges into character-building opportunities. Let Christ's mindset guide you (Philippians 2:5). Anticipate good things from God's goodness."

Seeking God for Victory and Joy

"Have a Great Day Today! Turn to God for victory over life's struggles (2 Peter 1:3). Overcome temptations by asserting your spirit's control over emotions (Galatians 5:16)."

www.ingramcontent.com/pod-product-compliance
Lightning Source LLC
Chambersburg PA
CBHW050758160726

48004CB00002B/607